Sean Kenney

Cool Robots

Christy Ottaviano Books

Henry Holt and Company

New York

For Mom and Dad

Henry Holt and Company, LLC
Publishers since 1866
175 Fifth Avenue
New York, New York 10010
mackids.com

Library of Congress Cataloging-in-Publication Data
Kenney, Sean.
Cool robots / Sean Kenney.
p. cm.
ISBN 978-0-8050-8763-5 (paper over board)
1. Robotics—Juvenile literature. 2. Robots—Juvenile literature. I. Title.
TJ211.2.K45 2010   629.8'92—dc22   2010007350

First Edition—2010 / Book design by Elynn Cohen
LEGO bricks were used to create the models for this book.
The models were photographed by John E. Barrett.
Printed in China by RR Donnelley Asia Printing Solutions Ltd., Dongguan City,
Guangdong Province

5 7 9 10 8 6

Let's build some robots!

Welcome to Robotopolis!

This is a busy city full of robots and spaceships.

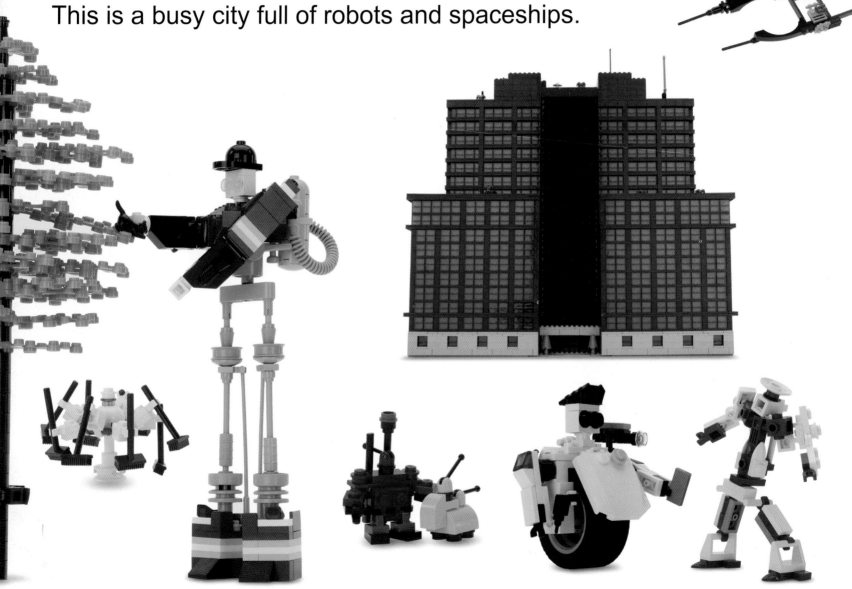

Family life

Even robots like to enjoy an afternoon at home.

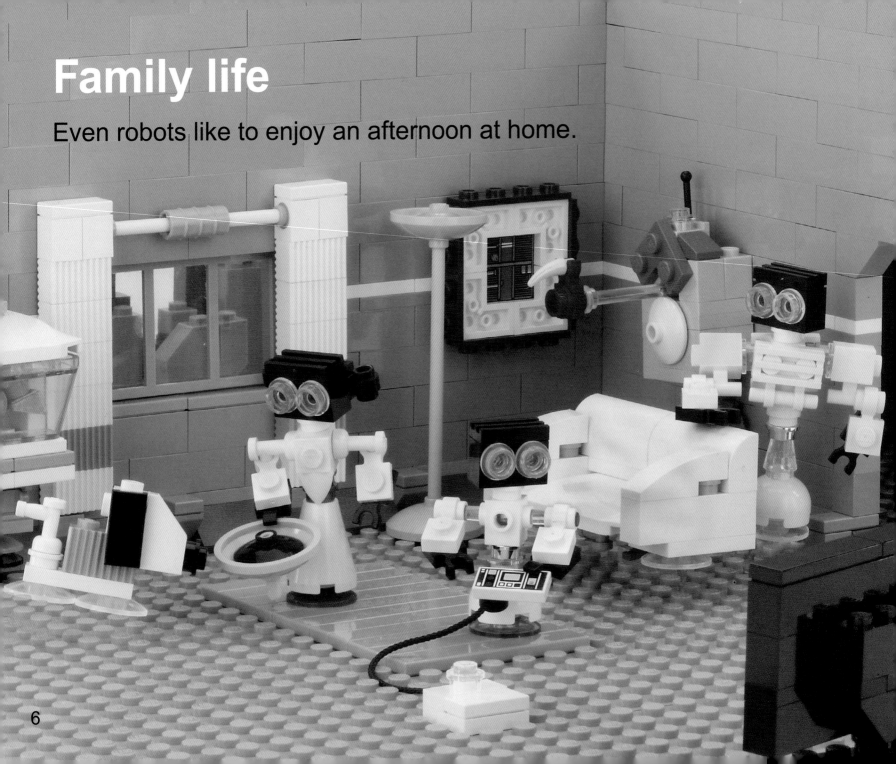

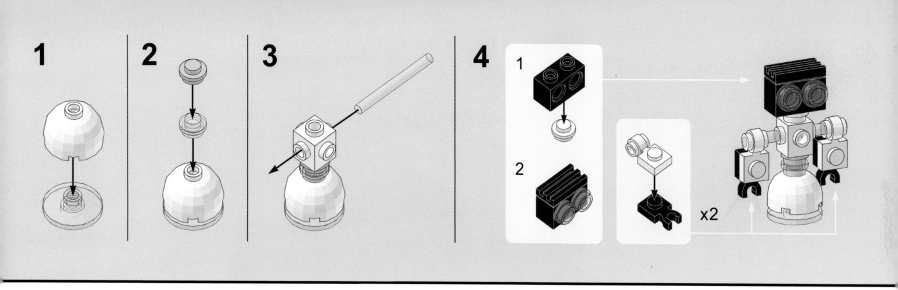

1

2

3

4

1

2

x2

Can you build the rest of the family?

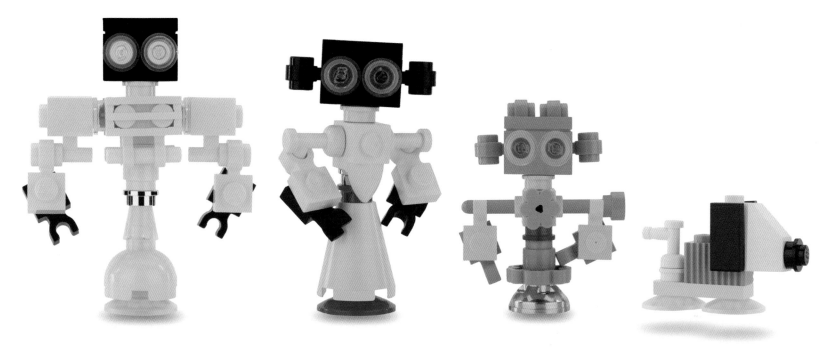

Across space, across town

Most robots get around town in a flying car.

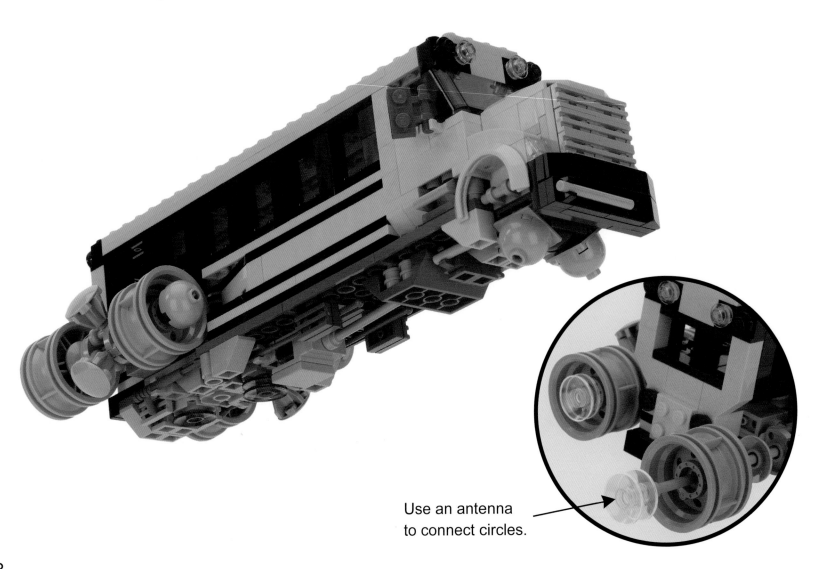

Use an antenna
to connect circles.

Turn any car into a hovercraft by taking off the wheels and adding cool space parts.

What other kinds of flying cars can you make?

Let's build!

You can build your own city of robots and spaceships.

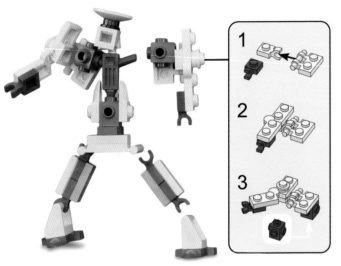

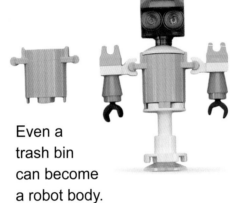

Even a trash bin can become a robot body.

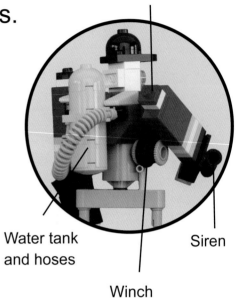

Emergency lights

Water tank and hoses

Siren

Winch

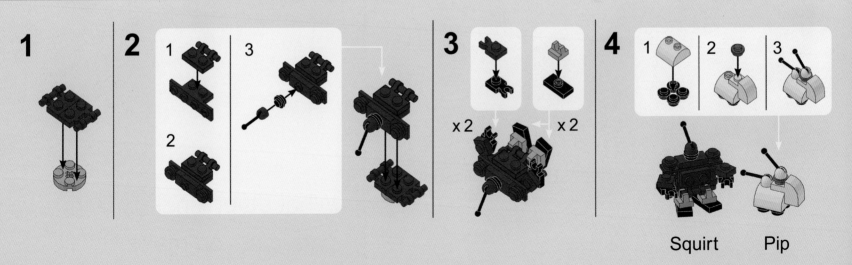

Squirt   Pip

1

2

3

4

5

6

1

2

3

7

No arch piece?
Try this:

=

=

8

1

2

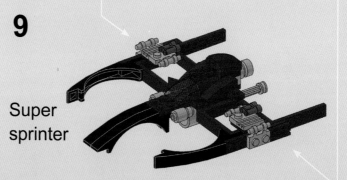

1

2

3

4

1

2

3

4

9

Super
sprinter

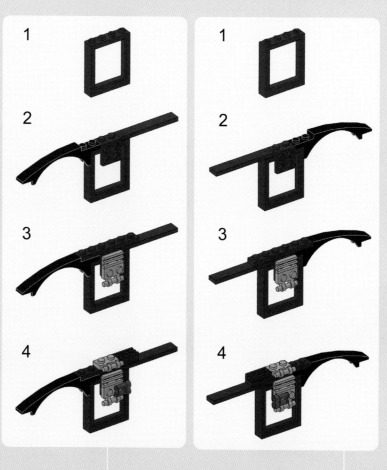

11

Special delivery

This truck changes into a robot and delivers its own packages.

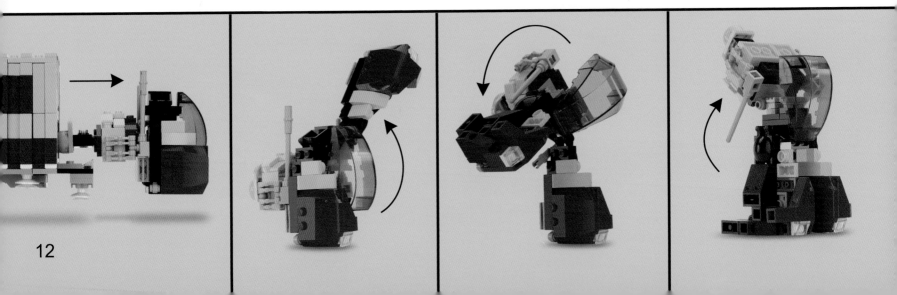

Build a bot

Mix and match your own pieces.

Middle

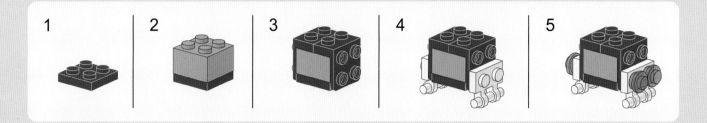

1   2   3   4   5

Use whatever parts you have.

Feet

Use a clip on top.

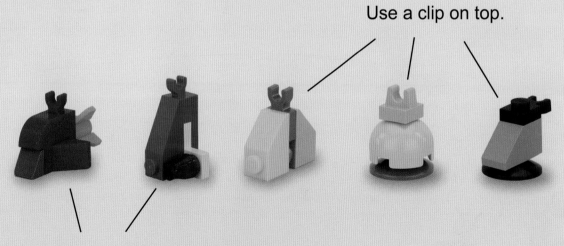

Make them wide to help your robot stand.

Arms

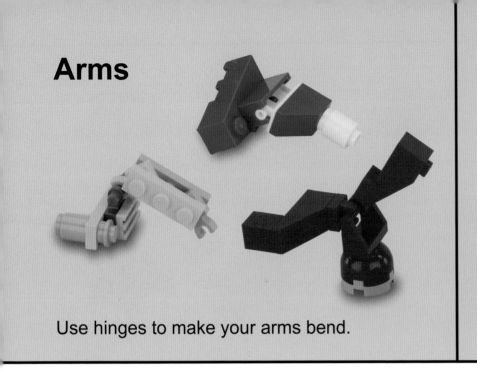

Use hinges to make your arms bend.

Heads

Put it all together

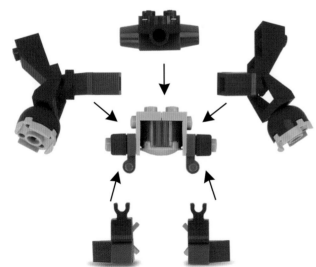

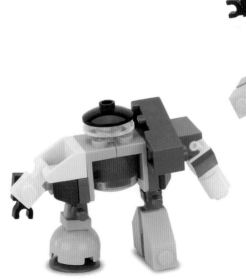

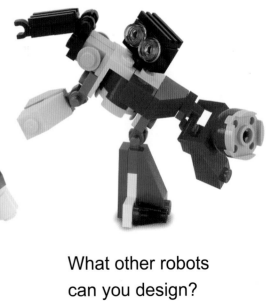

What other robots can you design?

Flatten it down

Build a mosaic to create a flat picture of a robot.

Strong bots

Big, tough bots help protect Robotopolis
from the forces of evil.

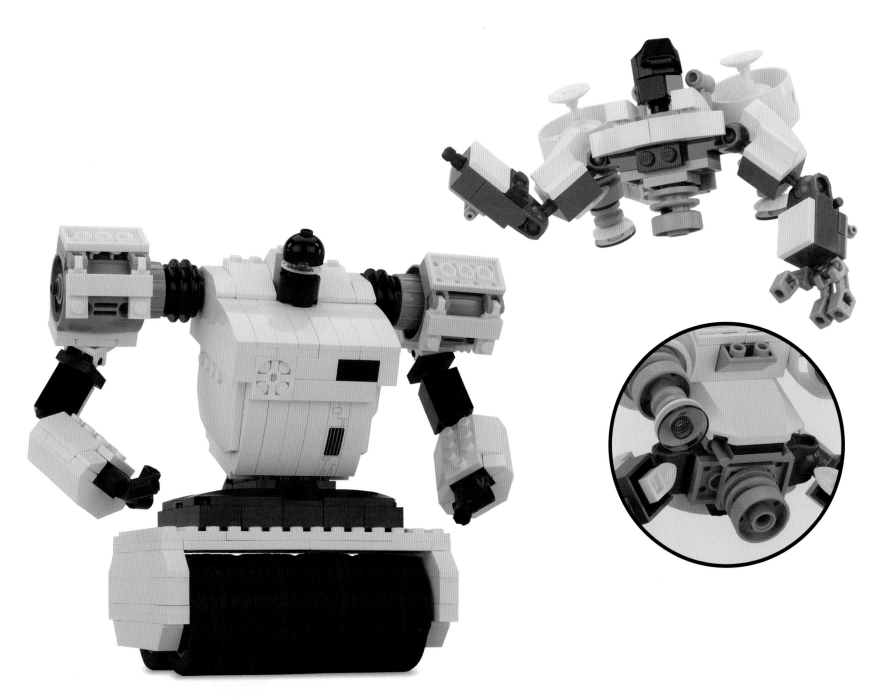

Pocket-sized crazy bots

You only need a few pieces to build a community of robots.

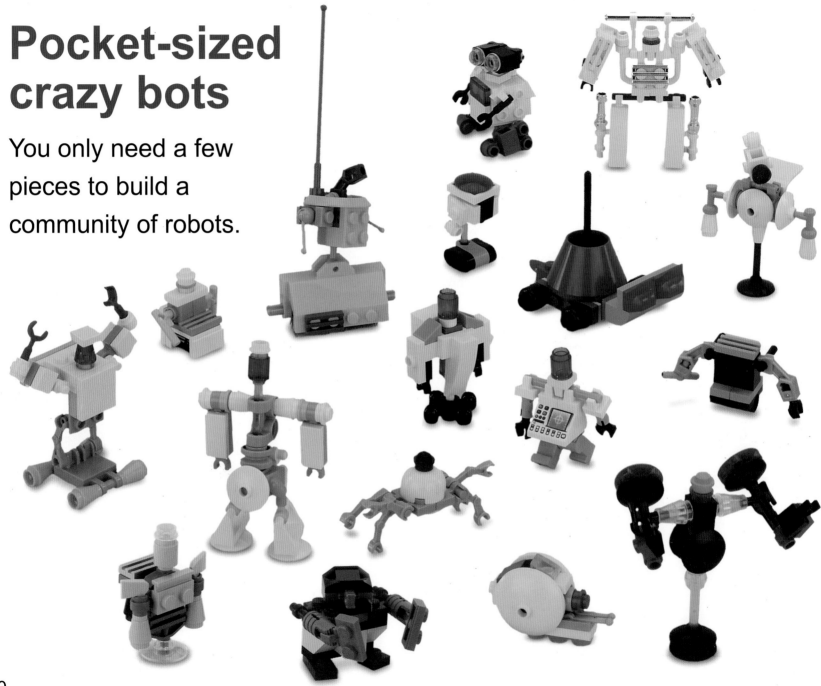

1

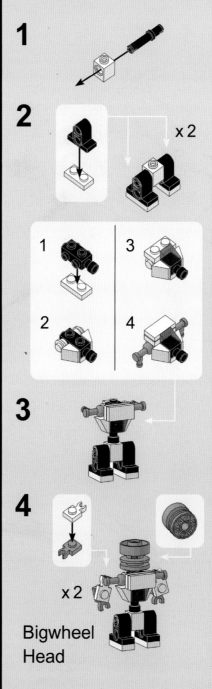

2

x 2

1	3
2	4

3

4

x 2

Bigwheel
Head

1

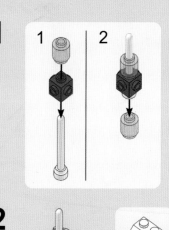

1	2

2

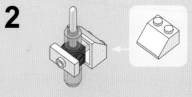

3

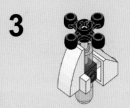

1	2	3

4

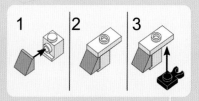

x 2

Shoulderlert

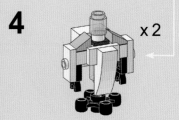

21

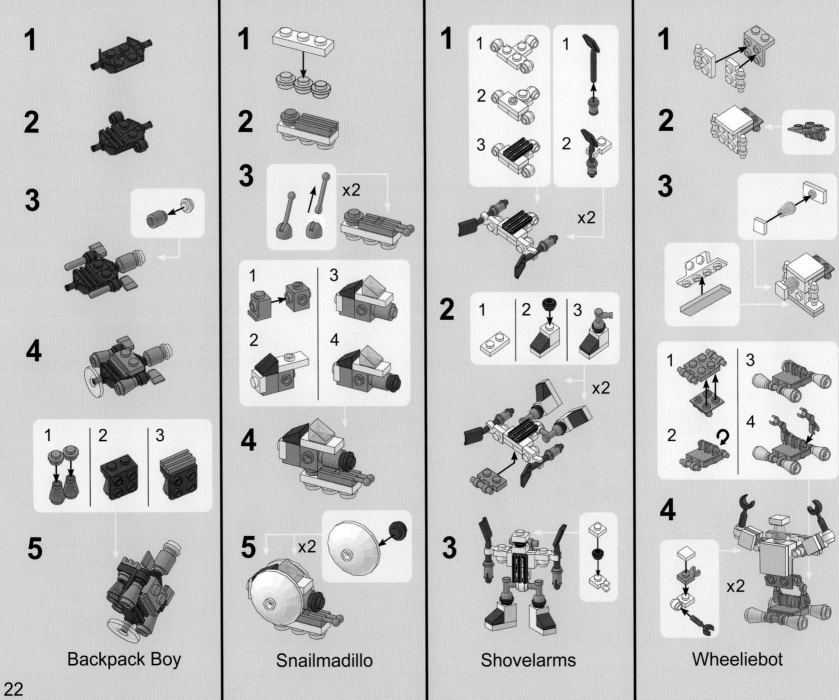

1

2

3

4

1 | 2 | 3

5

Backpack Boy

1

2

3

x2

1 | 3
2 | 4

4

5 x2

Snailmadillo

1

1
2
3

1
2

x2

2

1 | 2 | 3

x2

3

Shovelarms

1

2

3

1 | 3
2 | 4

4

x2

Wheeliebot

22

Build it BIG!

Make jumbo-sized pieces, then combine them into a giant robot.

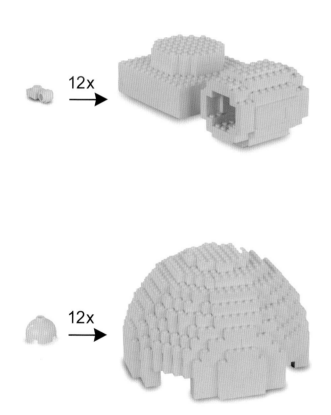

12x ➔

12x ➔

Building Robotopolis

These robots are a construction worker and a tough truck, all in one.

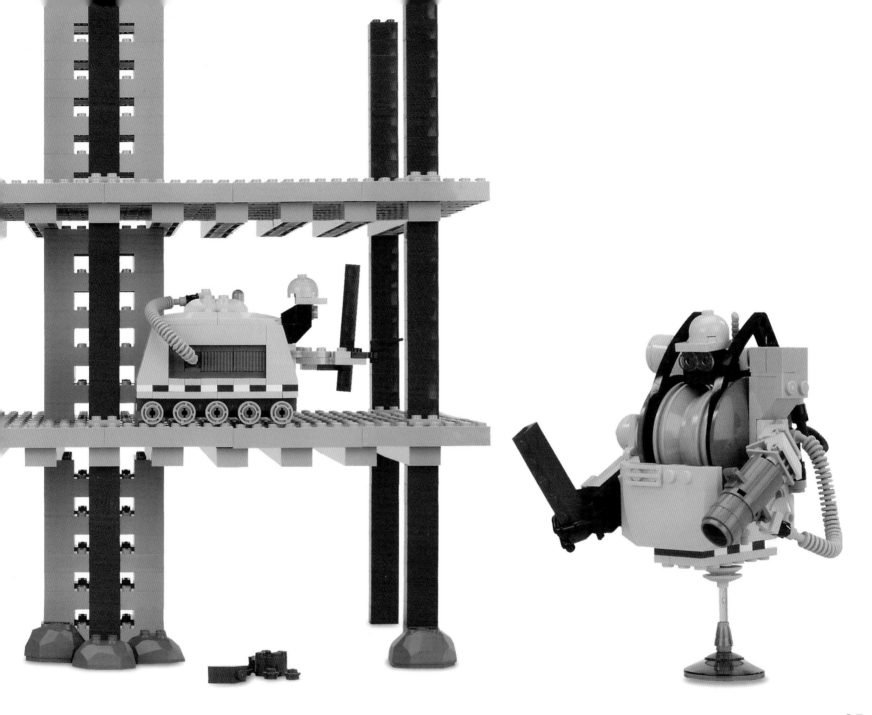

A tiny fleet

If you don't have enough pieces to build lots of large spaceships, try making them in a smaller size.

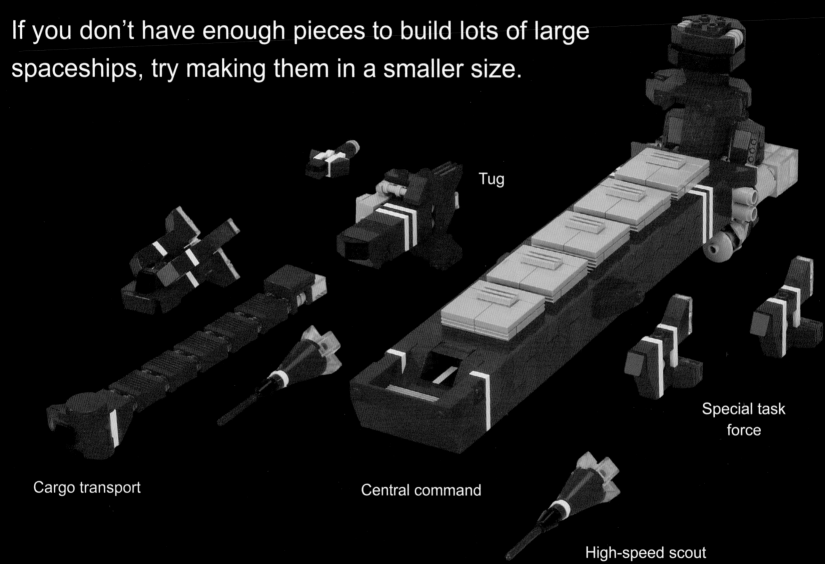

Tug

Special task force

Cargo transport

Central command

High-speed scout

Get creative with tools

Accessories make great robot parts.

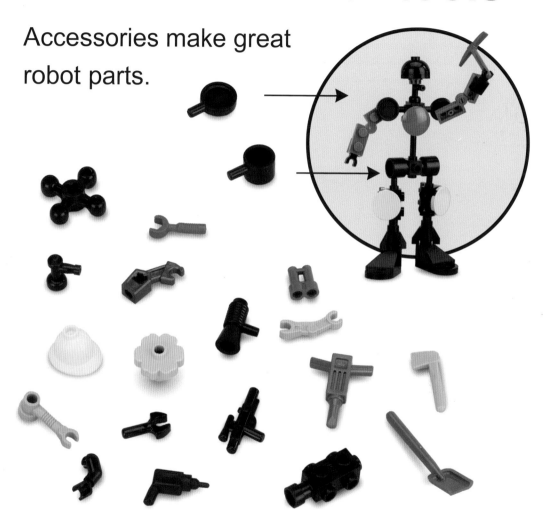

Recon shuttle

General-class sprinter

Can you find where these parts are used in this book?

Take a break at the space station

Traveling through outer space can take a while.

Why not stop along the way?

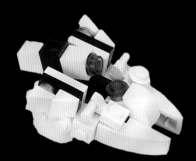

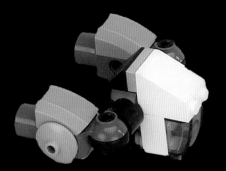

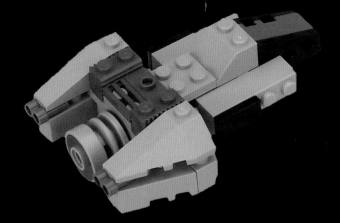

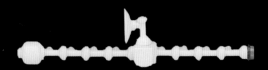

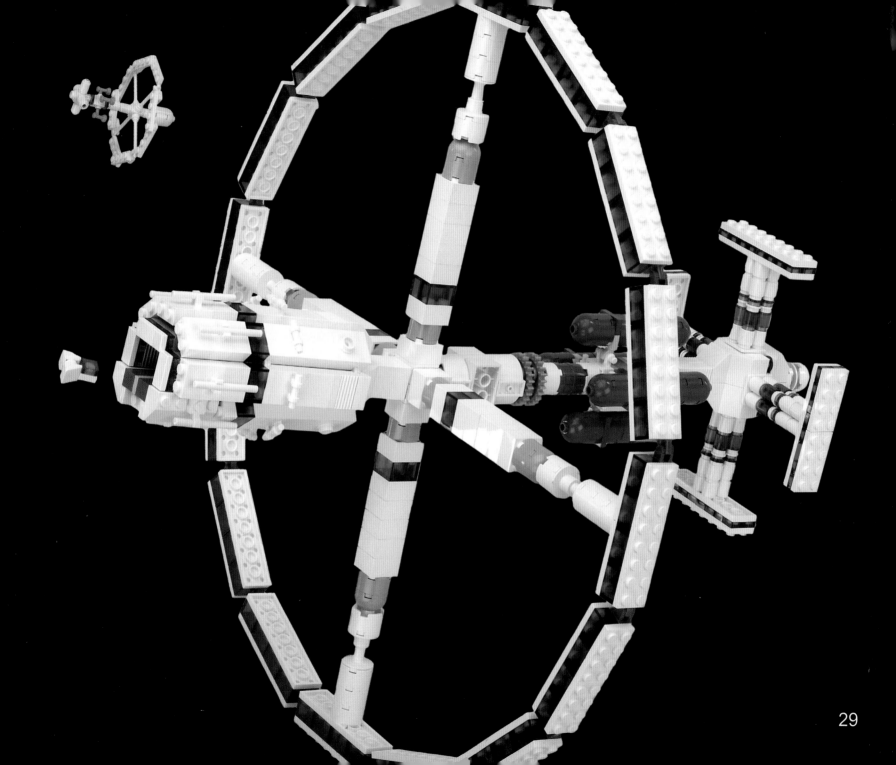

Time to relax at home . . .

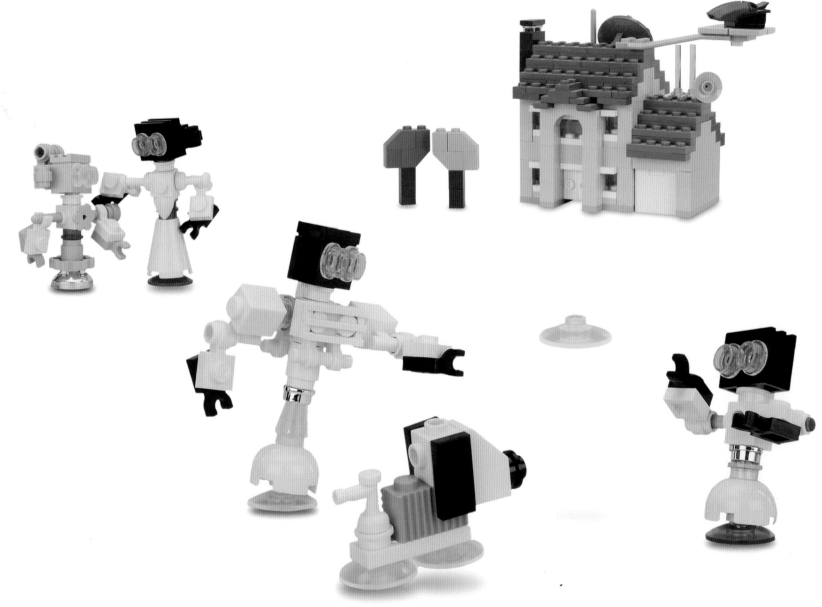

until the next adventure!

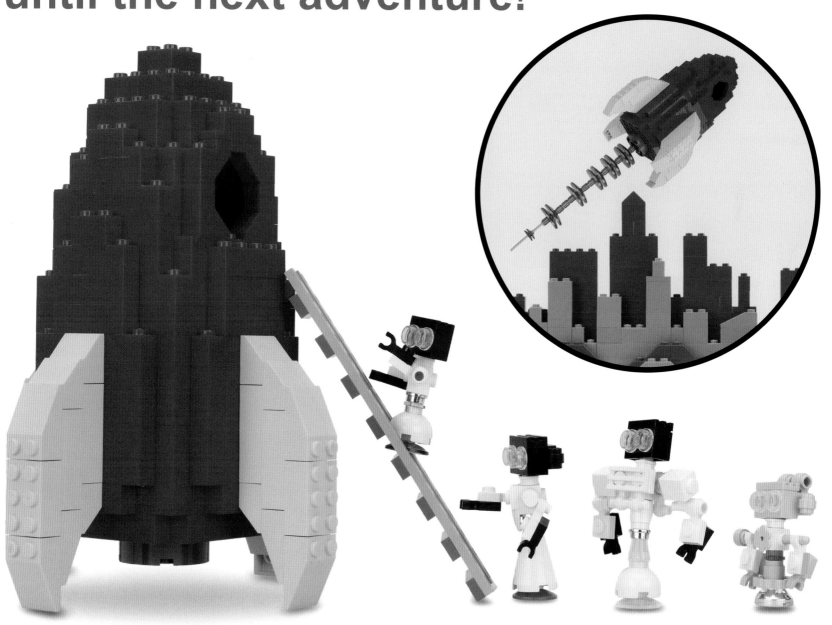

About Sean

Sean Kenney is a LEGO Certified Professional. He likes to prove you can build anything with LEGO bricks. He makes sculptures and models at his studio in New York City.

Sean picked up his first LEGO bricks as a child, and his passion for LEGO grew through the years as he grew. He is now recognized as one of the premier LEGO brick builders in the world.

Visit Sean at www.seankenney.com to:

- Share your cool robots with kids around the world
- Order some extra LEGO pieces
- Find out if Sean is coming to your neighborhood and more!